SOUL✝GOOD

Daily Devotions
Volume II

SOUL GOOD

Daily Devotions
Volume II

N'spired Hands

I want to give thanks to my Heavenly Father,
for anointing, appointing, and approving me.
Lord, you have inspired me with peculiar hands to
write yet another book. I am NOTHING without you
and to you be the glory. – Nicole Mathis

Introduction

Beloved,

I wrote this book to inspire you to "stop in the name of love," the love of God. This is Volume II and I want to encourage you again to not be so busy with life that you do not spend time, daily, with our Heavenly Father.

Like Volume I, this is a 31-day devotional to encourage your time with our Heavenly Father and to encourage your meditation on His Word. For each day, I have provided a menu of fresh "food" for you to ingest. Read the daily "menu" item with an open heart and mind. Then, think on what you have taken in and journal whatever is on your heart. Use this devotional to reflect and meditate on the blessings of God.

Blessings,

Nicole Mathis

Also known as

N'Spired Hands

Day 1

Soul food for the day, on the menu is - **Love**. Love is the greatest addiction. Love covers a multitude of sin. God is love. God gave us His ALL. Love does not change!!!
John 3:16; 1Peter 4:8

_____

_____

_____

_____

_____

_____

_____

_____

_____

_____

_____

_____

_____

_____

_____

Day 2

Soul food for the day, food for thought - **Let it burn.**
Lost soul catch on fire and burn with the holy spirit. All
about the kingdom, and souls. Preach, teach, and reach
the people. Proverbs 11:30

_____

_____

_____

_____

_____

_____

_____

_____

_____

_____

_____

_____

_____

_____

_____

Day 3

Soul food for the day, on the menu is - **Blessings on blessings**. "Dear friend, I pray all is well with you, and your healthy in your body, soul, as you are in your spirit." Overflow. Overflow. Overflow. 3 John 1:2

_____

_____

_____

_____

_____

_____

_____

_____

_____

_____

_____

_____

_____

_____

Day 4

Soul food for the day, on the menu is - **Give**. God has my back so there is no lack. Do not close your hand. Nothing from nothing leaves nothing. Open your heart, as well as your hands to give. The blessing will leave your hands but never your life. Remember, the more you give the more He gives to you. Be a cheerful giver. Luke 6:38

Day 5

Soul food for the day, on the menu is - **What are you hiding?**
U lie
U smoke
U drink
U cheat
U gay
U homeless
U a hoe
U tired of being alone
U kill (watch your mouth)
U steal

U think you done so much wrong that God can't use you. STOP in the name of love. Jesus know all about the problems/issues you have. Take ALL your heavy loads to the Lord and leave them there. Stop hiding and seek God while He may be found. Cast all your cares, issues, heavy load, and the struggle is real on Him. Make a U-turn. You can change, if you want. Isaiah 55:6-7; 1 Peter 5:7

Give Me You

God is not a man, so He does not lie. He is not human, so He does not change His mind. Does He speak and then not act? Does He promise and not fulfill? The Lord your God

Is with you, the Mighty Warrior who saves. He will take great delight in you; in His love He will no longer rebuke you, but will rejoice over you with singing.

Verily, verily I say unto you, He that hears my word, and believes on Him that sent me, has

Everlasting life and will not come into condemnation; but is passed from death unto life. Come to

Me, all you who are weary and burdened, and I will give you rest. We all, like sheep, have gone astray,

Each of us has turned to our own way; and the Lord has laid on him the iniquity of us all. For my

Yoke is easy, and my burden is light. For the word

Of God is living, active, sharper than any two-edged sword, piercing to the division of soul and of spirit, of joints and of marrow, and discerning the thoughts and intentions of the heart. Blessed is the man who perseveres

Under trial, because when he has stood the test, he will receive the crown of life that God has promised to those who love him.

A.A.A.

Day 6

Soul food for the day, on the menu is - **Wisdom**
Walking
In
Salvation
Depending
On the
Most High God.
Wisdom is Supreme. Proverbs 4:7

_____

_____

_____

_____

_____

_____

_____

_____

_____

_____

_____

_____

_____

Day 7

Soul food for the day, on the menu is - **Think Big**.
Believe
In
God
One faith. One Lord. One baptism.
Who is above all? Who sees all? Who created all?
Ephesians 4: 5-6

_____

_____

_____

_____

_____

_____

_____

_____

_____

_____

_____

_____

_____

_____

Day 8

Soul food for the day, food for thought - **Pieces of Me**. Like a puzzle that has many pieces, give God all the pieces until you're broken. Allow yourself to heal. In return God will give you peace that surpasses all understanding. It is okay to be broken, but gracefully. Philippians 4:7.

Day 9

Soul food for the day, on the menu is - **Choose to love**. It is so amazing to be loved. Like a rose, a seed has to be planted. Over a period of time, it blossoms into a beautiful flower. A red rose symbolizes confidence, passion, and sacrifice; Christ did all of that for us. God planted a seed for a beautiful flower to blossom. God loves us; but do we love him? God requires **L.O.V.E** in return!!!
1st John 4:8

Listen to
Our
Voices
Every day in prayer

Day 10

Soul food for the day, on the menu is - **Make a deposit.**
Nothing from nothing leaves nothing. The foundation
must be solid like a rock. Your foundation has to be from
the ground up. You have to build it up. You must make a
deposit in order to get a withdrawal. Your account will
show insufficient funds until there is a deposit.
Deposit your time. Deposit your body. Deposit your soul. Deposit
your spirit. Deposit your trust in God. Deposit something into your
heavenly account, daily. Matthew 7:24-27; Colossians 3:23

Day 11

Soul food for the day, on the menu is - **S.T.O.P**
Standing on
The
Omnipresent
Promises of God
2 Corinthians 1:20

_____

_____

_____

_____

_____

_____

_____

_____

_____

_____

_____

_____

_____

_____

Day 12

Soul food for the day, food for thought - **Get a seed in the ground**. Why? Sow seeds where you're being feed. Harvest time must come. Psalms 37:25

Steal Away

Study and do your best to present yourself to God approved, a workman [tested by trial] who has no reason to be ashamed, accurately handling and skillfully teaching the word of truth. But someone not knowing does

Things worthy of punishment will be beaten with few blows. From everyone who has been given much, much will be required; and from him to whom much has been committed, more will they ask of him. But let a man

Examine himself, and so let him eat of that bread and drink of that cup. For he who eats

And drinks, eat and drinks judgment to himself if he does not judge the body rightly. For this reason, many among you are weak and sick, and a number sleep. For if we would not judge ourselves, we should not be judged. I will

Lift up my eyes to the hills. From where does my help come? My help comes from the Lord, who made heaven and earth!

And my God will meet all your need according to the riches of His glory in Christ Jesus. I must

Work the works of Him that sent me, while it is day: the night comes, when no man can work.

As long as I am in the world, I am the light of the world. Let not

Your heart be troubled. You believe in God; believe also in me. In My Father's house there are many mansions. And if not so, would I have told you that I go to prepare a place for you? When everything is ready, I will come and get you, so that you will always be with me where I am.

A.A.A

Day 13

Soul food for the day, food for thought - **Your love is king.** My first love and my last love always will be My King. Romans 8:38-39

_____

_____

_____

_____

_____

_____

_____

_____

_____

_____

_____

_____

_____

_____

_____

Day 14

Soul food the day, on the menu is - **D.E.B.T**

Doing
Everything
But spending
Time with God.

Two hours and forty minutes in a day is ten percent of your time.
Make time for God. Matthew 6:33

_____

_____

_____

_____

_____

_____

_____

_____

_____

_____

_____

_____

_____

_____

_____

_____

Day 15

Soul food for the day, on the menu is - **Beware**.
When something is fake it looks real and may even have a
shine. Over a period of time the true color will appear.
People can deceive you as well; watch them dogs. Beware
of wolves in sheep coverings. Philippians 3:2

_____

_____

_____

_____

_____

_____

_____

_____

_____

_____

_____

_____

_____

_____

Day 16

Soul food for the day, on the menu is - **Queen Me**
While he is stroking you up and down and you're enjoying
the pleasure principal, please know your worth!!!
Every time you lay your body down, you're walking into a
marriage without a covenant/promise. This is for the
lover in you! Put a sign up, saying, "Do not enter; you're
trespassing." This is my promise to you; sex is a gift of God for those
who are married. Remember, snakes will not enter into the kingdom
of heaven. **NO WED: No BED. QUEEN ME**.
Hebrews 13:4; 1 Corinthians 6:18-20

_____

_____

_____

_____

_____

_____

_____

_____

_____

_____

_____

_____

Day 17

Soul food for the day, on the menu is - **New Season**
Behold I am doing a new thing!!!

Reunited
Renewed
Revived
Recover
Restoration
Refreshed
Released
Restart

In order to go to the next season/chapter, something must come to an end. All about the Kingdom. It is a new season. Isaiah 43:19; 2 Corinthians 5:17; Ecclesiastes 3:1-9

_____

_____

_____

_____

_____

_____

_____

_____

_____

_____

_____

_____

Day 18

Soul food for the day, on the menu is - **Power Up**
The blood will NEVER lose its power.
It sanctifies.
It purifies.
It dignifies.
It satisfies.
It justifies.
The Blood still works!
Hebrews 9:22; 1 John 1:7; Luke 22:20

_____

_____

_____

_____

_____

_____

_____

_____

_____

_____

_____

_____

_____

Day 19

Soul food for the day, on the menu is - Live your life like it's **G.O.L.D.E.N.** Here and now I choose to live more, laugh often, and love always. **Love Always Win**.
Ephesians 5:19; Hebrews 10:25; Ephesians 4:15

Give an
Offering of time
Love &
Devotion
Encouraging self
N the Lord daily.

_____

_____

_____

_____

_____

_____

_____

_____

_____

_____

_____

_____

_____

Day 20

Soul food for the day, on the menu is - **Hell No**. People say, I rather be safe than sorry. I totally agree. Be safe in the arms of the Lord. You lived your best life. Now, you realize it is too late: you're in hell lifting your eyes. You faithfully made excuses and entertained the father of lies. Hell is real; a place you do not desire to go. Open up your heart. Allow God into your life, and tell the devil **HELL NO.** Deuteronomy 30:19; 1 Corinthians 15:33; Isaiah 5:14

Clean This House

Call me, God I need to talk to you. It has been a very long time.
Lord, I do not know what to do. Now, I want to lean and totally
depend on you. So many tears: I cry myself a river at night. Why is the
Light not shining: like the son which is so bright? It seems like
Every path I choose are no wins, you just loose. I need to hear
A word from a friend, someone who will
Not lie to me or set me up. I been many places, and

Tried many things. I
Have looked for love in all the wrong places.
Is heaven so far away that my cry is never heard? I NEED YOU
NOW. I need to hear a word. Lord, I need your help. My hands are in
the air. I surrender all.
Say a word, please. I give you permission to come into my

Heart, body, mind, and soul. I
Open my heart up to receive you. I am blind, and do not
Understand. I repent of all my ugly sin. Lord, please take my hand.
Show me the way. I am nothing without you.
Every knee must bow; even Satan his self. Every tongue will confess
that you are the Lord, Jesus Christ.

Day 21

Soul food for the day, on the menu is - **Fly Like An Eagle.** When people are watching you like a hawk, spread your wings and just fly away. I can do all things through Christ which strengthens me. I BELIEVE. Fly like an eagle: with them eagle eyes. The anointed soul that could. Isaiah 40:31

_____

_____

_____

_____

_____

_____

_____

_____

_____

_____

_____

_____

_____

_____

_____

_____

_____

Day 22

Soul food for the day, food for thought - **Fight On: Grow On**. In the kingdom of God a fight was started. The violent bullies were arrested and thrown out by warriors of God. If you are going through hell; come out on fire. We have not because we ask not. As people we have the authority to ask God to set you on fire so you may burn for Him; like a consuming fire. Remember, the anointing destroys, breaks, beat, the yoke. It is the little foxes [which are distractions] that comes to steal, kill, and destroys the vine [which is growth] like a plant or spiritual. Choose to be a warrior of God who is anointed, appointed, and approved by God. Isaiah 10:27; Matthew 11:12; Song of Solomon 2:15

Day 23

Soul food for the day, food for thought - **Out of Control**
You cannot act like a devil and stand behind God. You
cannot live wrong and die right. 2 Corinthians 6:14;
Galatians 5:19-21

Day 24

Soul food for the day, on the menu is **- C.O.F.F.E.E**
Christ
Over
Family
Friends
Everyone
Everything
Remember, like a good cup of coffee: **Hebrews**. John 14:6

_____

_____

_____

_____

_____

_____

_____

_____

_____

_____

_____

_____

_____

_____

Day 25

Soul food for the day, on the menu is - **SPIRIT & TRUTH.** Jesus is the real deal: He is the only way to make it today. John 8:32; John 4:24

Serving
Purpose
In
Righteousness
In
Truth
&
Turn
Repent so
U do not go
To
Hell

_____

_____

_____

_____

_____

_____

_____

_____

_____

_____

_____

Day 26

Soul food for the day, food for thought - **Hurt people hurt others**. If you cannot build a person up: stop tearing them down with your mouth. Words hurt like sticks and stones. Proverbs 18:21

_____

_____

_____

_____

_____

_____

_____

_____

_____

_____

_____

_____

_____

_____

_____

Day 27

Soul food for the day, on the menu is - **Do Not Quit**.
Anybody may be recruited as a soldier. A warrior of God
endures and does not quit: know the difference.
Ecclesiastes 9:11

_____

_____

_____

_____

_____

_____

_____

_____

_____

_____

_____

_____

_____

_____

Day 28

Soul food for the day, food for thought - **U better think**. People do not be deceived. Hell is real: Jesus is real. Yes, people do not take God serious enough at His word, and that is pretty sad. If you die tonight, where would you spend eternity? God has given all who choose to come to Him through His son, Jesus Christ: eternal life. This brings all humanity to the place where each of us must individually make a choice. Will you accept or reject the call? You have a free will to choose life or death. Love always wins: open up your heart allow Jesus in. You have not because you are not asking. Remember, you cannot live wrong and die right. Isaiah 5:14; Psalms 9:17

Day 29

Soul food for the day, food for thought - **Wait 4 Love**.
Whoever does not love does not know God because God
is love.
Above all, love each other deeply, because love covers
over a multitude of sins.
If you love me, you will keep my commandments.
Those who love their children care enough to discipline
them. Three things that are too wonderful for me;

For which I know not: how eagles fly so high, a snake moving
on a rock; a ship finding its way over the sea, and the way of a
man with a virgin. A new commandment I give you, that you
love
One another: just as I have loved you, you should love each
other. Now these three
Remain: faith, hope, and love: but the greatest is love.

Love never fails. Let the words
Of my mouth, and the meditation of my heart, be acceptable in
your sight, O Lord, my strength, and my redeemer. Favour is
deceitful, and beauty is
Vain: but a woman that fears the Lord, she will be praised. Be
humble, then, under the powerful hand of God, he may
Exalt you in due time. Give all your worries and cares to God,
for he cares about you.

_____

_____

_____

_____

_____

_____

Day 30

Soul food for the day, food for thought - **R.O.S.E**
Beautiful like a rose: Be U 2da fullest. Like a rose, nothing is wasted. I went from withered to winner.

Rejoice in the Lord always and again I say rejoice.
Oh come let us adore him.
Shalom. It is written: "As I live," says the Lord,
Every knee will bend to me and every mouth will open to give praise to God."

Reaching
Others
Souls
Effectively

Remember, the flower girl places rose pedals down the aisle, so the Queen can be taken to the King. Song of Solomon 2:1

_____

_____

_____

_____

_____

_____

_____

_____

_____

Day 31

Soul food for the day, food for thought - **N'spired Peculiar Hands**. May the work I have done in earth speak for me. Proverbs 31:31

_____

_____

_____

_____

_____

_____

_____

_____

_____

_____

_____

_____

_____

_____

_____

What You Shame Of?

Preachers don't preach like they use to, just let the members do what they want to do.

The tithes and offering as well as the people belong to God not you.

Why are you pleasing man instead of God?

What You Shame Of?

We say we representing Jesus then lift his name up.

Members don't give like they use to. I have to get my hair and nails done, and by the way my rent is overdue.

God knows my heart.

What does it profit a man to gain the whole world and lose his soul?

Hell is real, and a place you don't want to go.

What You Shame Of?

Do not fall in love with Jesus because you may fall out of love with him as well.

Grow in love with Jesus and tell the devil no your soul is not for sale.

There are only two places you may dwell: for some heaven, and others a burning hell.

What You Shame Of?

Today, people want to play house. She is the cheese and you are the mouse: want the milk for free: but will not marry me.

What You Shame Of?

God is love. His love comes from heaven above. The right thing to do is to be sold out for Jesus: like a hand and a glove. Let him be the lover of your soul. Say yes, and stop saying no.

What You Shame Of?

A.A.A.

Other books by the Author

Soul Good Daily Devotions

Soul Good Daily Devotions Volume I is filled with words that will captivate your mind like food does to your taste buds. This book offers encouragement, garment of praise, words of wisdom, inspiration, and food for thought. Are you ready to eat? Nicole put this book together carefully, with love, beauty, and faith. Get ready to be fed and have your soul encouraged for 31 days. It's not just good, it's *Soul Good*!

Available on Amazon.com and Walmart.com

All About Love

In this book of poetry, Nicole Miller gives more than 10%. She writes and shares her heart about love – love for God and love for others. Nicole is an overcomer who has learned the power of choice. She chooses to live more, laugh often, and love always. In this book, **All About Love**, Nicole plants a seed for love to blossom in your life.

Available on Amazon.com

ALL
ABOUT
Love

NICOLE MILLER

Pretty Sad

Pretty Sad is an anthology about the extraordinary strength of women. In Volumes I, II, and III of this powerful series, women from all walks of life have come together to expose every bruise, wound, and hurt from their past. In Volume IV, the mask and the makeup have been removed as the following women face themselves and their truth: Arisha Nabors, Colette Toomer Cruz, Fotima Hall, Freida Lorraine Queen, Jennifer Corona, Keci Monique, Latonya Littlejohn, Melissa McGill, Natasha Robinson, Nicole Miller, Shanea Farr, and Lead Author Tanya DeFreitas. Grab your tissue and follow along as these women tell the truth, the whole truth, and nothing but the truth!

Available on Amazon.com

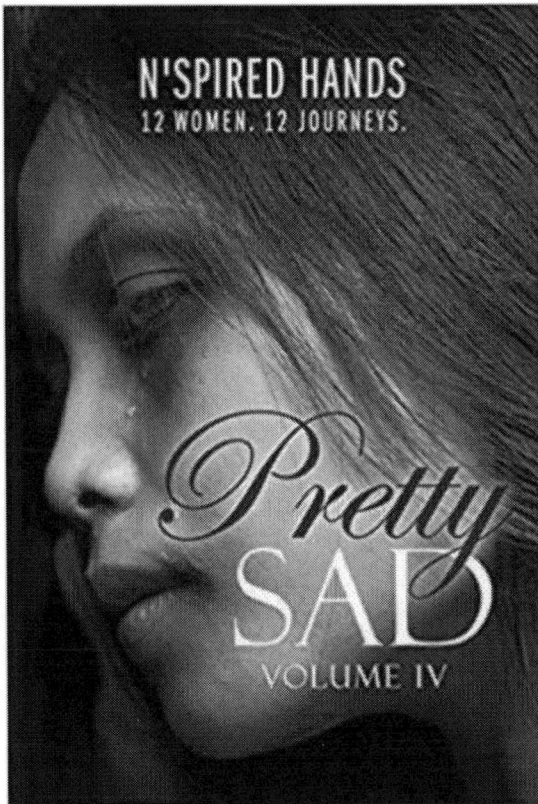

Made in the USA
Las Vegas, NV
03 November 2021